YOU Could Be a Better Father

7 Steps to Having a Better Father/Son Relationship God's Way

By Hansen Harper
Father's Edition

By Hansen Anthony Harper

Copyright © 2017 The Awakened Company.

All rights reserved. No part of this book or any of its contents may be reproduced, stored in a retrieval system, or transmitted in any form or by any means, electronic, mechanical, recording or otherwise, without the prior written permission of the author.

Printed in the United States of America.

Scripture quotations marked (AMPC) are taken from the Amplified® Bible (AMPC), Copyright © 1954, 1958, 1962, 1964, 1965, 1987 by The Lockman Foundation. Used by permission. www.Lockman.org

Scripture quotations marked (KJV) are taken from the King James Version. Public domain. http://www.BibleGateway.com.

Scripture quotations marked (NASB) are taken from the NEW AMERICAN STANDARD BIBLE®, Copyright © 1960, 1962, 1963, 1968, 1971, 1972, 1973, 1975, 1977, 1995 by The Lockman Foundation. Used by permission.

Scripture quotations marked (NIV) are taken from THE HOLY BIBLE, NEW INTERNATIONAL VERSION®, NIV® Copyright © 1973, 1978, 1984, 2011 by Biblica, Inc.® Used by permission. All rights reserved worldwide.

Scripture quotations marked (NKJV) are taken from the New King James Version®. Copyright © 1982 by Thomas Nelson. Used by permission. All rights reserved.

Scripture quotations marked (NLT) are taken from the Holy Bible, New Living Translation, copyright © 1996, 2004, 2007 by Tyndale House Foundation. Used by permission of Tyndale House Publishers, Inc., Carol Stream, Illinois 60188. All rights reserved.

The author is providing this book and its contents on an "as is" basis and makes no

representations or warranties of any kind with respect to this book or its contents. The author disclaims all such representations and warranties for a particular purpose

The author will not be liable for damages arising out of or in connection with the use

of this book. Using the information contained within, you agree not to hold the author liable for any loss or injury caused by acting on such material or suggestions contained herein.

Editing services by www.ChristianEditingServices.com.

Styling by A.J. the Barber of Headquarters Barbershop, Houston, Texas.

Photography by Al Torres Photography, Houston, Texas.

Printing by Disk.com

I would like to dedicate this book to two people. The first is my father, Floyd A. Harper. Dad, you always kept me by your side and taught me what being a real God-fearing man was all about. Though you were frustrated at times with me and my ways, as a father you continually poured Christ, character, and servanthood into me. I appreciate and love you for investing time, whether in sports, church, school, or life. You have always been an enthusiastic fan of mine. Dad, I love you. You're my best coach ever!

Second, I would like to dedicate this book to my only son, Zion Caleb Harper. Coauthoring this book with you has been my greatest joy and honor. You are so bright and intelligent, and you love the Lord with everything you have. From the day I held you in my arms as a baby to now seeing you becoming a young man sprouting up before my eyes, it has always been a privilege to be your dad. It is because of the great and godly example I had from my own dad that I am able to pass that legacy down to you. You are one of my greatest accomplishments. Zion, you are my MVP!

Your son/father,
Hansen A. Harper

Contents

Foreword   7

Preface   11

Acknowledgments   13

1. Critique Freak   15

2. Attendance Does Not Mean You're Present!   21

3. You're Looking at You!   25

4. Slowly Let Him Go!   31

5. No Doesn't Mean I Don't Love You!   37

6. Your MVP   41

7. The Perfect Father   49

Father Talk   57

Foreword

You Could Be a Better Father: Seven Steps to a Thriving Father-Son Relationship God's Way by Hansen Anthony Harper is a dynamic new book that helps us fathers learn how to do an even better job at fulfilling the parenting roles for which God designed us. Although every Christian father should want to do a great job in raising godly children, we struggle with many kinds of obstacles: work, relationships, health, and finances, for example. Sometimes we're just too tired or too busy to invest in our sons the way we should.

When they are based on a Christ-centered foundation, father-son relationships have the potential to transform the world in this day and age when society is changing very rapidly for the worse. In this phenomenal guidebook, Hansen demonstrates how fathers can and must become the beacons of light their sons need to create an unbreakable bond that will last a lifetime and beyond, into eternity. He helps dads better understand their sons from the unique perspective a father is given from our heavenly Father. His book also guides fathers to stronger bonding opportunities between them and their sons.

Each of the chapters in *You Could Be a Better Father* holds up a mirror to every father so that he can see himself as others view him. Readers will discover common parenting mistakes, like misjudging a son's actions as disobedience when they sometimes spring from other causes, such as misunderstanding or avoiding public embarrassment. Fathers can readily identify with scenarios presented in this book so they can begin to change themselves in God-honoring ways before beginning to mold their sons in the same design.

Based on God's Word as the ultimate and only reliable parenting manual for all generations, *You Could Be a Better Father* not only identifies common errors made by fathers but also explains how to stop making them. In the chapter "Critique Freak," for example, we are reminded of the temptation to over-criticize our sons when correction should be balanced with praise and appreciation. The "Lessons I Learned" section at the end of each chapter offers simplified concepts to benefit readers. A "Buddy Builder" section provides easy-to-do tips for helping fathers apply the principles outlined in each chapter. The concepts are easy to grasp and formatted in a readable framework that even the busiest of dads can still find time to read in just a few minutes each day. Every father could learn (or relearn) important and treasured principles for raising sons to love God and serve him even in the midst of family life. Indeed, becoming a positive role model for young boys who closely follow their fathers' examples is likely the most important goal any father could hope to accomplish in this world and especially at this time in history.

My ministry in Kingdom Principles has reinforced the importance of godly family leadership as the center of God's will and purpose for this world. This kind of leadership begins in the home. A man who cannot manage his own family is unprepared to serve as a leader in other areas, whether it be at his job, in his church, or within his community. Men and fathers, we are to look out for our families' well-being and teach our sons how to put the needs of others ahead of their own. As our boys grow up, they need to know how to serve God. They also need to know how to be godly leaders in their homes when they marry and how to be godly fathers to their children to raise them to walk in righteous paths (Psalm 1). There is no greater goal than to raise up our children in the way they should go (Proverbs 22:6) and to do so in a way that brings honor to God. Learning to become an effective dad can involve years of trial and error. Hansen's book helps fathers become more aware of their needs and limitations and offers many insightful shortcuts sidestepping pitfalls, overcoming weaknesses, and trusting God in this crucial area while learning how to praise, guide, and discipline sons in meaningful ways.

Quality time spent in learning how to be a good dad and then becoming one is one of the best investments a Christian man can make during his lifetime. I'm grateful to know a father like Hansen Anthony Harper, whom I encouraged for several years to share his knowledge and experience by writing a book for dads who want to do the best job possible in raising their sons in the Lord. He writes with a sincerity that is hard to find in other parenting books, even those written from a Christian perspective. The author's close relationship with God is the pivot point for this work on the important topic of father-son relationships.

All who reads this book are sure to enhance their understanding and appreciation of Christian fatherhood and the human struggles we face on a daily basis. With the help of Hansen's book, fathers can start applying useful principles immediately to enjoy a more wholesome and fun relationship with their sons.

APOSTLE HENRY ABRAHAM
FOUNDER AND CEO
CHRIST-CENTERED MAN INTERNATIONAL

Preface

In this day and age, we see many troubled father-and-son relationships. Dads are absentee or just human ATMs. Dads are not equipped to handle the demands of the millennial son. Sons are being led and entertained by so much technology that they have traded the very voice of their dads in for Facetime, Snapchat, Instagram, and so on. With earbuds constantly in their ears, they have tuned out the rest of the world except for whatever they want to focus on at a particular time, and dads have very few biblical comebacks. The days of fathers and sons just simply going fishing, doing yard work together, taking in a ballgame, or painting the fence at home are long gone.

Well, with this double book from a father-and-son perspective, I want to bring those old days back! There was substance to those activities such as going to the barbershop together or sitting down and taking in a baseball game while stuffing your face with a hot dog. It was an honor if your dad said, "Hey, son, do you want to hang out with me today in the garage?"

You would just about break your neck trying to spend time with your dad. How about playing catch? Ah, the good old ball and glove. My dad and I spent countless hours playing catch. He always kept a bat, ball, and mitt in the trunk of the car, so if we wanted to kill time or happened to go to the park, we had all the necessary equipment readily available.

This double book gives fathers and sons an avenue and outlet to experience godly fatherhood and sonship together like never before. Each chapter has a story and encouraging word for fathers and sons. And then the best part of each chapter is that it has a distinct and fun activity for fathers and sons to do together. My son and I want to bring God, fun, and functionality back to fathers and sons in the kingdom of God with some down-to-earth tips, tools, and advice that will take your father-son relationship to the next level! Even if you are without your biological father or are standing in for a boy's father, this book is for you.

I am honored that God would select me to write this book with my son, Zion. We hope to change the terrible condition of fatherhood and sonship in the kingdom of God one father-son relationship at a time! My challenge to every father and son who reads this book is to get all your Buddy Builders done within the next six months and record enjoying each other. Your father-son relationship is destined for greatness in Jesus Christ's name. Amen! Let's have fun!

Acknowledgments

I want to thank my mentor and founder of Christ-Centered Man International, visionary and leader of Kingdom First Ministries, Apostle Henry Abraham. I would like to acknowledge my loving wife of twelve years, Dionne Harper, who has continually supported me in my endeavors to add value to other people through my books, coaching, and keynote speaking. I am a dreamer: I may have one new idea right now, and in the next four minutes I have a whole other set of brand-new ideas. Through the years, my wife has learned to hear my dreams and then rationalize them down to doable bite-size pieces, and I appreciate her for that. Thanks, Babe. I also acknowledge my parents, Floyd and Ovellia Harper; my in-laws, Ruby Douglas, Reverend Sam Douglas, and Mary Douglas; my brother and sister-in-law, Reverend Craig Barnett and Donna Barnett; and Reverend Ord Limbrick and Angela Limbrick. Special thanks to all the other family and friends who have supported me through the years.

Critique Freak

Ephesians 6:4: "*Fathers, do not provoke your children to anger by the way you treat them. Rather, bring them up with discipline and instruction that comes from the Lord*" *(NLT).*

Dads! Come on! Turn to that handsome dad next to you and ask him, "Who do you know who's a critique freak?" Think about it. . . . Think about it. . . . Got that guy in your mind? Good!

You know who this guy is! He is the loudest, most annoying, inconsiderate, rude, argumentative, bullyish, disrespectful, graceless, abrupt, blunt, impolite, intrusive, uncivil, insulting, unrefined, and disagreeable guy you have ever seen! Even more than that, in my experience I have seen this already out-of-control guy absolutely leap off the pages when his son disappoints him. No matter how hard the son tries to please his dad, everything the son does is met with a verbal or physical lashing.

Yeah, this guy is terrible. But you know who else can be a critique freak? You and I. Let's face it, dads: we have all played this role in some way at times. Come on—you know you have! You whip out humiliating phrases such as "What's wrong with you?" or "I wish you were more like_____." You tell your son, "You're such a disappointment," or "I'm going to stop wasting money on you." Even better: "You're definitely from your mom's side of the family," "Quit crying like a little girl," or "You're a waste of my time."

Dads, seriously, how many of you are guilty of saying some version of these statements? Well, I'm guilty of saying some of these words to my son, and let me tell you, they are very hurtful and destructive to any father-son relationship. They eat away at the enamel of your father-son relationship, and if they aren't stopped, your son's self-image will slowly but surely be destroyed!

I know, gentlemen. Our problem as critique freaks is that we want to criticize and micromanage our son's every move, leaving no room for originality, personality, growth, or teachable moments. But the question remains: Why do we critique freaks get like this from time to time? Well, let me be honest with you. There are some things our sons do that just drive us up the wall! That is the time when the critique freak comes out. You tried to suppress the critique freak monster all day, but your son keeps doing this annoying thing—let's say he's popping his gum loudly while your family's out somewhere—

in spite of your giving him chance after chance. Your wife has even run interference between you and Junior all during the trip, but for some reason your son didn't get the memo. It might not bother anyone else that your son pops his gum in public, but for you, this is the last straw! Now it's time to let your son have it, right?

Before you answer that question, let me give my own example. My critique freak moment happened when my son, Zion, and I were going to volunteer in a local Vacation Bible School one summer. During the school year, Zion has to tuck his uniform shirt in for school. I get that. But during the summer? Come on, man! No good boy—or man, for that matter—should be bound and wrapped up with his shirt tucked in. Anyway, we were exiting the house, and to my extreme dissatisfaction, I looked back and saw Zion had his shirt tucked in so snugly. I was infuriated. I had warned him several times about how I wanted him to be loose and comfortable when we went out. Talk about critique freak!

When we got to VBS, I looked back at Zion again, and, lo and behold, he had that shirt tucked back in again! I was really about to go off, but instead I asked him calmly, "Son, why is your shirt tucked in again after we've talked about this a thousand times?"

He simply responded, "Dad, my shirt is too big, and I don't want people laughing at me."

Wow! It was that simple. In that moment, I had an epiphany. I remember how it was to be laughed at as a child, and I would make adjustments to avoid embarrassment just as Zion did. Even as adults, we'll do practically anything to avoid embarrassment. My approach was that my son was going to make me look bad at VBS, but in his mind, he didn't want to look bad. His shirt was just too big, so he tucked it in the way he was used to doing! Reflecting back on my own dad and having compassion on Zion, I reassured him that if he just loosened up, nobody would even notice his shirt. Well, just as I predicted, when we stepped through the doors of VBS, nobody even noticed how long his shirt was. Zion was a hit with the other kids, and he had fun!

In hindsight, I was able to process what happens to us critique freaks at times. Our overly aggressive and public critiques of our sons can tear their spirits to shreds. We have all heard the phrase "It's not *what* you say but *how* you say it." This is especially true when it comes to communication with our sons.

I used to be a major critique freak. Let's get this straight: I didn't really think I was all that bad. However, I learned to recognize the first sign that dads have a problem with criticizing their sons too much: When your son does one awkward thing, how do you react? Do you go totally off? Do you rip him to shreds because you're trying not to be embarrassed by the "untucked shirt," as I did?

I'll never forget Zion's basketball game when his team totally blew out the opposing team. Walking out after the game, I saw a boy from the opposing team leaving with his mom and dad as well. According to the brute gestures and level of intensity in the dad's voice, he was obviously very upset. As we got outside, this dad began cursing his son out. The mother (as mothers often do) was playing the referee. You know how it goes: "Calm down, honey! It's just a game! Why don't you give it a rest? He's only ten years old!"

But as you well know, her attempts only ticked off this critique freak dad more. He yelled more curses in his son's face. The son was totally dejected, and the worst thing is, he looked back at me with tears in his eyes as if he were my son. At that moment, I saw myself in the boy, and I knew I had to change my critique freak ways toward my own son. I vowed that day that I would become a catalyst for father-son relationship reform, especially within the church.

Believe it or not, dads, our sons have a breaking point. God has placed us as stewards over our sons for a short time. We're going to have to give an account for how we handled them. I asked myself a question one day, and you can ask yourself the same question as well: "What if God dealt with me the way I deal with my son?"

If God himself hammered down on us as hard as he could, who would be able to handle that? We dads have done so much deserving of punishment and death, yet God had mercy on us. Psalm 103:13 says, "Just as a father has compassion on his children, so the Lord has compassion on those who fear him" (NASB). Without God's mercy, dads, you see how messed up we would be? Let's all agree right now that with the Lord's help, we're going to put to death the critique freak in all of us through actively monitoring not only what we say to our sons but also how we package our words.

I believe in you, dads. I decree and declare that the critique freak is broken in you right now and that the power of the Lord Jesus Christ holds your spirits up as we invest time, talent, and treasure in our sons. In Jesus's name, Amen!

Lessons I Learned

- Words really do have power!
- We are stewards over our sons for a short time. We will be held accountable to God for our dealings with and treatment of them.

Buddy Builder

Right now, find three positive things to say about your son, and tell him these things face to face over a meal.

Attendance Does Not Mean You're Present!

Ephesians 5:15–16: "Look carefully then how you walk! Live purposefully and worthily and accurately, not as the unwise and witless, but as wise (sensible, intelligent people), making the very most of the time [buying up each opportunity], because the days are evil" (AMPC).

One day I had come home from a long, hard day of work as a teacher when Zion asked me for help with his homework. Instead of being overjoyed about the opportunity to help my son, I had an attitude. My wife, who is a teacher as well, was helping our daughter, Zoe, with her homework. I had hoped I would find some peace at least at my own home, but it was the exact opposite. My wife needed this; the kids needed that; the job needs blah, blah, blah. I just wanted be left alone. Just my being in the house should count for something, right, dads?

Sometimes as fathers we are so irritated or tired from work, but we show up to our homes, and we are on time! We think somehow we deserve credit for doing this. On the contrary! Our attendance does not mean that we are actually present, fully engaged, and there for our kids. I shouldn't have been irritated with my son when he asked for help with his homework. After all, I do spend the majority of my time helping strangers' kids when I teach during the school year. Shouldn't I have even more patience when it comes to my own kid?

As a teacher, the number one thing I try to get my seventh graders to do is actively participate in their learning. Several studies have shown that the more people participate in an activity, the more likely it is that they are to learn. On my worst days of teaching, I have students who do show up to class, but when I call on those students to answer a question, they say, "Huh? What did you say?" They are in attendance but not present!

Dads, isn't that how we are sometimes with our sons? We say, "Yeah, uh-huh, good job, Buddy," but we have no clue what's really going on with our sons. We must present our sons with all of us and not be just in attendance. Remember: if you halfway spend time with your son, that time will be lost forever.

I'll never forget that hot summer day when I was in the house lounging aroung looking at a TV show, and Zion asked me, "Dad, could we go play on the Slip 'N Slide in the backyard?" Man. Here we go again! I just wanted to relax. But instead, I mustered up all my strength to spend time with Zion. I pulled out that Slip 'N Slide, and Zion and I ended up having a blast!

That afternoon is one of his fondest memories of our spending time together. I wasn't just in attendance—I was present.

The point I'm trying to make, dads, is that by doing something as simple as playing on a Slip 'N Slide with Zion, I was there physically, mentally, and spiritually for my son. Right on that Slip 'N Slide, I was able to listen to his hopes, dreams, and fears as we laughed and had plain old fun. Because I put time into our relationship, I got so much in return.

Fathers, I challenge you today to find more time in your lives to be present and just not in attendance with your son. This prioritization is especially important for the dads who are not in their sons' homes due to divorce or separation. All the more, don't penalize your son because you have issues with your ex. Treasure the times you do share.

While I do realize that we dads are leading busy lives with work, ministry, committee, boards, coaching, and so on, we must violently fight to find the time to dedicate to and be present with our sons. Find those Slip 'N Slide moments with your son as I did. There is no greater joy for both you and your son than to know that your son's presence is not a burden to you but a blessing. Don't just be in attendance—be present!

Lessons I Learned

- Father-son relationships are healthiest when you make yourself present physically, spiritually, and emotionally.

- Father-son relationships work like putting money into a bank: if you put nothing in, you get nothing out.

Buddy Builder

Purchase tickets to a game, monster truck rally, concert, rodeo, or other event that would be fun for you and your son. Make a really big deal about it. Get matching shirts; buy snacks; do it up! And lose the cell phone, guys. Remember, dads: be present!

You're Looking at You!

Psalm 103:13: "Just as a father has compassion on his children, so the Lord has compassion on those who fear him" (NASB).

What does your son do that really annoys you? The list can go on and on. Does he chew with his mouth open, tuck his shirt in, wear his cap nonstop, sing offkey, dance weirdly, scratch his head, drink straight from the milk carton, perform practical jokes, cry, mouth off, rave and rant, cheat, steal, lie, act lazy, or make excuses? Yeah, go find the nearest mirror and stare for about sixty good seconds. Finished? Who do you see?

I have a little secret to tell you. When you look at your son, you're looking at you! Have a little compassion, dads. Our sons do the things we often forget we did when we were their age. I remember when my parents flew out to Houston for the first time to visit us for Christmas. After hugs and kisses from Zion and Zoe, my mother wanted to take a picture with them. As I went to take pictures, Zion kept making these really goofy faces on purpose. I began to yell at him to stop. After hearing about all he could take, my dad cut in. "Hansen, you used to do the very same thing when we wanted to take pictures of you." I debated and denied the charges until my dad kept telling story after story after story from my childhood. I really did do some of the same things. Go figure.

It's amazing how we dads have selective memory about our childhood blunders. As a consequence, we hold our sons to this perfect standard that we've never reached, but then we turn around and expect our sons to be flawless.

Zion plays center for an AAU basketball team called Total Package. Zion is big and tall for his age, and as a center he has to be tough. This past season he played in a tournament in Dallas, and the opposing team had boys who were just moving Zion out of the way and going to the hoop. They weren't bigger than Zion, but they played with heart and were fearless. Needless to say, Zion and his team got blown out. I knew Zion had much more in him, but I think he buckled under pressure. I wished he were tougher.

I'd invited my cousin Kelsey from Dallas to see Zion play, and he also said that Zion needed to be more physical and toughen up. Kelsey is an ex-drill sergeant and a retired police officer, and he can be a bit of a loose cannon. He ended up giving Zion different pointers about how to be tough and telling him stories about his life. Then he told Zion to try to hit him. Of course, Zion didn't really want to do it. I was standing back just watching to see how tough Zion was. He came at Kelsey and tried to do a move or two but quickly buckled under Kelsey's years of expertise. Zion slipped and fell straight to the ground. At that point, I knew Zion had had enough of the tough stuff lecture, and I called Kelsey off. It was all in good fun, or so I thought.

All of a sudden, I flashed back to my relationship with my dad. When I played little league baseball, my dad always told me that I should be tougher and should try not to cry so much. Like Zion, I was always bigger for my age and looked older, but I just wanted to be accepted.

Then I had another mind shift. I remembered how my dad used to tell me stories about his childhood. He told me he developed his sense of toughness by looking at my grandfather's toughness. When my dad was a boy back in the 1950s, he got just whatever time he got with his dad. There was no sitting down and letting him cry and express his feelings. "Be a man" was the order of that day. As I reflected, I was pretty sure three generations of Harper men never intended to break the spirits of their sons. But in some strange way, they did. Right then I was convicted. Zion was me. Would I treat my son any better than I was treated by my dad?

On our way back to the hotel, I finally snapped back to reality and apologized to Zion. I didn't apologize for talking about toughness but for driving the nail into the wood so hard that the wood was on the verge of splitting. The truth is, dads, that most of the time we're looking at ourselves through our sons. We're usually trying to make our sons into something we never were ourselves. While I was giving Zion these tough lectures, I remembered I was never anywhere near tough. I wanted everyone to be my friend, and I hated confrontation. As we drove, I told Zion the truth about when I was his age. I shared with him that I was a lot like him when I was a kid. I told him my dad threw around that "Be tough, and be a man" phrase a lot. I let him know I just didn't want anybody taking advantage of him. I then apologized to him for being overbearing. Zion thanked me for what I said.

How about you, dad? Think about how your relationship with your dad affects your relationship with your son. Go back even further: how did your dad's relationship with *his* dad affect his relationship with you? You might be surprised to see how the past shapes how you treat and talk to your son.

The very behaviors or characteristics you get onto your son for not having are probably the same ones you wished you had at his age. Our insecurities end up being our sons' biggest persecutors as they venture on their journeys to manhood. We must break these generational curses by praying over our sons and encouraging them to read scriptures about who they are in Christ. Unless we purposely intercept ideals, images, and negative feelings of ourselves, our sons will surely reap worse than we ever had. So, dads, the next time your son does something that really irritates or embarrasses you, just do the following:

As yourself, "Did I use to do that?" (James 1:24)

Respond with grace and mercy (Proverbs 15:1).

Reassure your son of his identity in Christ (Psalm 139:14).

Impact his life with your unconditional love and compassion (Luke 15:20).

Lessons I Learned

- Our sons' irritating habits likely mirror something we displayed in our own childhood. Have some compassion!

- Get rid of old negative clichés like "Toughen up!" and "Be a man!" They're titles our sons will never be able to live up to, nor should they have to.

- God has looked over and forgiven all our flaws. By his grace, we should be able to do the same for our sons.

Buddy Builder

You and your son cook dinner together. It has to be something from a recipe. Microwave stuff doesn't count; the two of you have to prepare a real dinner, something that requires you to add ingredients together and follow directions. This process will give you and your son time to enjoy just being around each other. Remember to keep it very fun and light. The most important part of this assignment is to show your son unconditional love and understanding.

4

Slowly Let Him Go!

Proverbs 22:6: "Train up a child in the way he should go, and when he is old he will not depart from it" (NKJV).

Oh, that's so scary! He's looking at girls now? He's actually taking the time to brush his teeth? My goodness—is that clean underwear he has on? Is that strange scent cologne or Pinesol? You've got it right, dads. Our sons are growing up, so we have to let them go!

I remember the first time I laid eyes on Zion. He was a big ten-pounder with beautiful, big brown eyes, and he screamed and cried so loudly that the doctor had to close the door!

When he was a little older, I used to tickle him, and he would come running back for more. We made up the craziest songs and laughed and laughed about them.

How about you? Do you remember your son's first step, his first words, his first day of kindergarden, his first Easter speech, his first basketball goal, or his first touchdown? Do you also remember the day when your son stopped wanting to hang out with Mom and would fight tooth and nail to hang out with you instead?

These memories are really hard to let go of, but the truth is, things are changing, and your son is growing up. I started learning this lesson when my son was still young. At that time, Zion loved to go to Chuck E. Cheese's. I had to follow him around everywhere he went like a private detective, because he didn't watch his coins, and when he did win, he would leave his tickets in the machine to be taken by other kids. I was so afraid of some other kid taking advantage of Zion that I hindered his ability to just be a kid by watching his every move. The next time we went to Chuck E. Cheese's, instead of lording over Zion, I just allowed him to have the run of the place with minimal interference. To my surprise, Zion didn't do too badly. Though he lost a few more tokens and tickets than I would have liked, he had a blast, and my Chuck E. Cheese's-induced stress was at an all-time low. I gave my son a little space, and I ever so slowly let him go.

In another example, Zion was invited to a sleepover with some of his cousins, but they were a few years older than Zion. I was very hesisitant because of some trust issues I had as a boy and because Zion was a lot less tough than his cousins. However, my wife finally convinced me to give Zion a little rope and let him have some fun at his aunt's house. Once my wife dropped

Zion off that night, I could hardly sleep; I was up worrying about Zion. I mean, I couldn't even release my own son to go to a children's sleepover at his aunt's? How pitiful was I?

That whole night I stayed up and pleaded with God to release me from this past hurt and to protect Zion. Believe me—his aunt had done nothing to warrant such a reaction from me. It was just my inability to get over my own past. Eight a.m. could not come fast enough. My wife and I hopped into the car, and I didn't know what I would find when we arrived at Zion's aunt's house. When we got there, to my relief all was well. Zion was playing and having a great time with his cousins. My fear was put to shame.

Now, dads, how much of your reluctance to let go of your son has to do with consequences of a bad experience in your past? The problem is (and I know it best) that your hurt, left unchecked, will end up jeopardizing and limiting your son's freedom and ability to make wise choices. Whether your issue is founded or unfounded, it could end up being your son's prison. When you realize your fears are limiting your son, seek counseling immediately from your pastor or another qualified person you really trust. I did, and it has really made a difference in my father-son relationship.

Dads, here's what I do know: if we slack off the rope just a little at just the right time, our sons will have a greater opportunity to enjoy their lives. Someone once said that life is the best teacher—we just buy the school supplies!

Now maybe your son isn't at that Chuck E. Cheese's stage anymore. Maybe he's at the first date stage. Maybe he's at the stage when he wants to stay over a friend's house without your supervision. Or maybe he's even at the stage when he's deciding what college to attend. Whatever the stage, we must learn to slowly let our sons go. As dads, and I know you guys will agree with me, we try to shield our sons from potentially hurtful and adverse situations as best we can, right? But the takeaway for us, dads, is that we're not God. There are some things our sons must go through that we as dads will not be able to save them from. If our sons never experience any type of adversity, then when it's time for them to leave the nest, they'll leave unprepared to be effective men. Give your son responsibility in pieces.

When I was very young, my grandmother would crack a wrapped piece of peppermint candy into pieces and hand the smaller chunks out to us grandkids to prevent us from choking. Well, one day I told my grandmother that I was a big boy and wanted the full peppermint. For whatever crazy reason, Grandma gave me the whole thing. I was happy as a mouse with cheese until I tripped over a pew and the peppermint ended up lodged in my throat. Once the deacons popped it out of my throat, I threw it away.

The next time my grandmother handed out peppermint, she asked me, "Hansen, do you want your peppermint cracked or whole?"

I immediately answered, "Cracked."

My sweet grandmother knew all along that a piece was all I could handle. The peppermint story provides a invaluable lesson for us dads. You see, Grandma never kept the peppermint away from me; she just gave it to me in pieces. Let's all do the same with our sons. Give them responsibility in pieces. Dads, let's all love, prepare, and protect our boys as much as possible and then slowly let them go!

Lessons I Learned

- We are not God.
- As much as we want to be there to protect our sons from all negativity, we can't.
- Trust the values you've instilled in your son.

Buddy Builder

All right, dads. This is going to take a little prep work on your part, because this is an outside event. For this Buddy Builder, you're going to need a pile of logs or bricks—about ten, no more than fifteen.

Instructions

1. Call your son out into the yard or field.

2. Give your son instructions to pick up all the bricks or logs at one time and walk them to point B, about fifteen feet from the pile. Your son will attempt to pick them all up at one time and will fail!

3. Ask your son the following questions:

   a. "Why can't you pick up all the bricks [or logs] at one time and move them to the end?" (He'll probably say because it's to heavy or too much.)

   b. "What could I do to help you to solve this problem?" (He's probably going to ask, "Could you help me?")

   c. You say, "Sure, but I'll only hand you the bricks [or logs]. You'll have to carry them on your own!"

The purpose of this Buddy Builder is to let your son know that you're there to support him but that, in real life, he's going to have to do some things on his own. You're letting him go slowly, but he's also growing up and learning to be responsible.

No Doesn't Mean I Don't Love You!

Proverbs 29:15: "The rod and reproof give wisdom: but a child left to himself bringeth his mother to shame" (KJV).

How many ways can we tell our sons no on a daily basis, dads? *Nope, Not today. Not this time. Negative. No way. Ask me later. Maybe another time. Not possible. Nah. Let me get back to you. Out of the question. No, sir. Not in a million years. Fat chance!* Just because we've said no to our sons in one way or the other doesn't mean we don't love them, right?

No real father wants to say no to his son for no apparent reason. As a matter of fact, most times we dads want to say yes to our sons if we have the means to grant their request. The only time we usually say no to our sons is to teach them a lesson, to protect them from danger, or to prevent them from hurting other people.

My mind goes back to my own father during my teenage years.

I was about thirteen, and all the craze in my town was about a teen club called "N-Effect."

All my friends had gone to the club and were bragging about what a good time they'd had. They were getting ready to go again, and I asked my dad. Dad flat-out said no! I was so hurt. I did so many chores, got good grades, and was active in church, and I couldn't go? Of course, I asked my dad the age-old question, "Why?" Dad just told me he had a bad feeling about that place.

The following Monday at school, I asked my friends what happened that weekend. They paused and looked at me. "You didn't hear? There was a shootout there, and a lot of people got hurt. A girl even got her faced sliced open with a box cutter!"

It was at that moment I really thanked God for my dad. His words sounded harsh initially, but his *no* potentially saved my life. What if I had been there? What if I were the one who'd gotten hurt?

Telling our sons no isn't a bad thing, especially if it's for a good reason. As a matter of fact, saying no can actually mean we love our sons. I think about Jesus in the garden right before his betrayal. Jesus pleaded with his father to take away the suffering he was about to go through. Even God told Jesus no, but his no was for redemptive purposes.

Let's praise God, dads, from the beginning until Jesus Christ returns for God the Father saying no to Jesus but yes to our redemption! It's because he loved his Son and us that he allowed

Jesus to suffer for us so that one day we would reign in heaven with him. Hallelujah for the no!

Lessons I Learned

- Telling our sons no from time to time is a good thing, especially if it's to protect them from danger.

- Saying no at times actually means we love our sons. No good father grants every request.

- God the Father's no to Jesus's request for the cup to be taken from him on the cross afforded us sinners a yes from God for redeeming our souls. Thank God for the no!

Buddy Builder

Take your son to work. Let him into your everyday routine and career. Let your son see what it takes every day to maintain your family's lifestyle.

If you can't let your son physically go to work with you, create your work environment around the home on one of your days off. Have him help you with tasks similar to what you have to do at your job. Then have lunch and discuss how your son felt being you for the day!

6

Your MVP

Matthew 3:17: "And suddenly a voice came from heaven, saying, 'This is my son, in whom I am well pleased'" (NKJV).

Come on, dads. When we think about our MVPs, we think about Peyton Manning, Aaron Rodgers, Michael Jordan, Kobe Bryant, Shaquille O'Neal, Cal Ripkin Jr., Landon Donivan, or Lionel Messi, just to name a few. After all, we build our fantasy teams and load them up with players to complement the MVP, right?

Let me ask you a question: How many of you have built your team around your Most Valuable Player—your son? Our sons need to have that special place in our lives; they need to know that we value, love, and respect them and that we're building our team around them for support.

I have three keys to help your son reach MVP status:

Key ①

For your son to become an MVP, he must be able to look up to you as a role model. When I consider people like Michael Jordan, Stephen Curry, Peyton Manning, or Lebron James, I have to remember that in order to play their positions as role models, these guys watch hours of film of the greatest players. They also had people in their inner circles who believed in them and invested time in them to achieve their goals. These athletes know the names, moves, and matchups of their favorite players for their sports.

Zion often does this very same thing with basketball. Shaquille O'Neal is his favorite basketball player. Zion is a big man just like Shaq, and he emulates Shaq's moves and habits during AAU games. Zion knows Shaq's stats and games in great detail.

Bringing this full circle, let's ask ourselves, dads: Do our sons know our plays? Are our sons our students? What do they see in our walk and our talk? Do our sons study our moves and plays? What plays have we been modeling for them? Have the plays been effective or ineffective?

The bottom line is that we should be the biggest superstar, other than God, in our sons' lives. Whether we believe they are or not, our sons are watching our every move.

One day I saw a commercial that really upset me. I have this little bad habit of talking back at the television. Anyway, I ranted on and on about it a long time. Later that day, I was in another room and heard this voice ranting and raving about something. I rushed to the living room, where Zion was ranting about a dumb play that a player had made during a basketball game. But instead of dropping it, he went on and on. I just stood back in astonishment at how my son would not let it go. And at this moment, of course, my wife looked right over at me with that wifely stare that says, "Uh, huh. Look at yourself!" Dads, you know what I'm talking about.

That day, I learned a very important lesson: to have our son at MVP status, we must ourselves be role models and maintain good behaviors. We have to stop lying, swearing, being hot-tempered, not spending quality time, critique freaking our sons—you fill in the blanks. All of us dads know those little things we do that our sons should never see and should not be done, period.

With our MVPs, we must be careful how we model the game of manhood. God, life, and society will hold us accountable for every good and not-so-good step we take. In order for our sons to be our MVPs and win the game, we dads must be worthy role models ourselves. Our sons won't do what we say—they will do what we model in front of them.

Key ②

In order for your son to become an MVP, he must be coachable. Studies have shown that some of the most successful coach-player relationships involve the player coming to trust the coach enough to correct his or her mistakes firmly but graciously. This change doesn't happen overnight. It is gained by the MVP/son knowing and trusting that the coach/father has a record of not only seeing his flaws but also correcting them with love, grace, and compassion, not with hostility and anger.

I experienced the effectiveness of this sort of relationship at one of Zion's basketball games. I noticed that he wouldn't jump up for the rebound. Instead of going right back up with the ball, he would bring the ball down to the ground, giving the little guards the opportunity to rip the ball right out of his hands. After the game, I recapped the game plan with Zion and showed him that as a center, when he gets the rebound, he needs not only to keep the ball high but also to jump right back up with the ball. Zion listened and applied what I said.

Once again, dads, I didn't give my correction in a mean or derogatory way. I came to Zion after the game, not in the heat of the moment. My mentor, Paul Martinelli, the president of JMT, once said, "Do not make your most important decisions in the valley—make them on the mountaintop." Correcting my son in the heat of battle used to be one of my biggest mistakes, but boy, have I learned. With this method, you should see dramatic improvement in your son.

Now Zion has progressed from two to four rebounds a game to eight to ten rebounds a game. I'm so proud of how coachable he's become! But remember, dads—we must correct our MVPs with an even and fair hand; that way, our MVPs won't tune us out. Let's continue to help our MVPs to remain coachable!

Key ③

Finally, in order for our sons to become MVPs, we must show them how to be committed to God. I've tried my best to be an example of God before Zion. First I woke up to read scriptures with him daily. Now Zion wakes up every morning and reads the Bible to his little sister, Zoe. He loves to go to church and gets excited about Bible study and anything that has to do with God. This excitement is very humbling. I've seen that if you train a child, a child will be trained.

Now, that works for both good and bad, dads. Modeling Christ before our MVPs is the most important seed we can plant. Dads, if you're lacking in your commitment to God, then your son is probably not consistent with his commitment either. We are the biggest Jesus our sons know.

Here are some suggestions to you dads to encourage your MVP's interest in Christ. You can fill his room with scriptures on the wall about God's promises. If he is into sports, get posters of Christian athletes, and plaster them all over his room. Go to your local Bible bookstore and let him pick out some cool Christian music, gear, games, or books he can relate to. Get him involved in an active and on-fire youth group.

These are just a few tips I've used for building my MVP status team. Remember, building an MVP is not going to be easy. However, with consistent modeling, player coachability, and God-centered focus, your son will be hoisting up that MVP trophy really soon. If it worked for my MVP and me, I know these three keys will work for you—but the ball is in your court now.

Lessons I Learned

- Our sons won't do what we say; they will do what we model in front of them.

- We need to remind our MVPs to remain coachable as we correct them with kindness at the appropriate time.

- Modeling Christ before our MVPs is the most important seed we can plant.

Buddy Builder

Pick any sport or game you and your son like. The object of the game will be that anytime your son scores, you will have to give him one positive affirmation and one constructive criticism. (Constructive criticism is criticism that builds up the individual. The opposite is destructive criticism, which destroys or breaks down the individual.)

So, for example, if my son and I have a free-throw contest, I might say that whoever makes the best out of five wins the game. The twist is, for every shot I make, I have to say one positive thing about my son's shot and one constructive critism. After you're done (not during the contest; remember, be present!), post your competition on Facebook, Periscope, or any other social media website. Have fun, dads, and enjoy time with your MVP!

Better Father
BETTER SON

The Perfect Father

1 John 3:1: "See what great love the Father has lavished on us, that we should be called children of God! And that is what we are!" (NIV)

For the most part, I think we dads try hard to understand our sons. More than that, we want to have an outstanding relationship with them. We long to grant their requests when reasonable (and sometimes when unreasonable). However, we're not perfect! I know I'm not. On our best days, dads, we fall totally short of what a decent father should be, let alone the perfect father.

Who here has a perfect father? No one! What does a perfect father look like? They don't exist!

The truth is that as natural dads, you and I mess up so much when we try to live up to a standard: the stern dad, the funny dad, the understanding dad, the take-no-prisoners dad, or the all-American dad. At best, we are poor versions of the only perfect father, God.

God is the perfect father because he gave his Son, Jesus a specific agenda while here earth. There are three things God did for his Son that for me checks all the boxes off to win the highest award for the perfect father.

God is the perfect father because he

① **Gave His Son Purpose**

> *For God so loved the world, that he gave his only begotten Son, that whosoever believeth in him should not perish, but have everlasting life.*
>
> — John 3:16 KJV

John the Baptist immediately identified the purpose of Jesus given by his heavenly Father (John 1:29). It was to take away the sins of the world. After the fall of Adam and Eve, humanity's holy relationship with God was eternally ruined. So God's plan for salvation was his Son, Jesus Christ.

On the earthly side, dads, if we just send our sons into this world without a sense of defined purpose, the world will substitute a counterfeit purpose that will lead to destruction. Just look at our daily news about our young men who are stealing, doing drugs, and confused about godly sexuality. These terrible things happen because young men aren't given a purpose.

One day at work about two minutes before clockout time, my boss called an emergency meeting. Nobody knew what it was about, and, frankly, no one cared. But let's turn that around. What if we were informed about the meeting days in advance and were given an agenda? Now, that would give us a clearer picture about what we should expect and what our responsibilities were.

One great way to give our sons purpose is to encourage them to pray daily and use their gifts and talents for God. Usually our sons' purpose is tied into the natural abilities God has given them. For example, my son's talents include community service. Since my wife and I are missionaries for Apartmentlife.com, about three times a month we must put on events for our residents and find a way to present Christ to them. Zion gets to see and participate in hanging out with and helping meet the needs of the people we serve. As a dad, I know his gifting. I just expose him to it. Now anytime Zion has an opportunity to use his talent of service, he does it with joy and knows that he is fulfilling his purpose.

That's one reason God is the perfect father: he exposed Jesus to his purpose and allowed him to fulfill his destiny. Let's do the same for our sons with God's help.

God is the perfect father because he

② Confirmed Purpose

When you confirm something, you declare that it's official and right. There were two major times in the life of Jesus when God confirmed his purpose. The first occurred when the angel appeared to the shepherds, letting them know that Jesus, the long-awaited Messiah, was born and that God's peace and goodwill had come to humanity. What a confirmation!

My dad tells the story of when I, his first son, was born. He waited in so much anticipation, and then, when I was finally born, he was overjoyed. We need to make sure our sons know how happy we are that they were born and that they belong to us.

The second confirmation happened when Jesus went to John the Baptist and was baptized. God spoke from heaven and told Jesus that he was loved and and well-pleasing. Dads, how many of us take the time to tell our sons how pleased we are with them? Most of the time we're too busy or even too embarrassed to do that. Positive confirmations from us dads always reassure our sons that they're on the right track.

Dads, let's start confirming our sons today. Don't just do it in your home or in private; affirm them in public. See how much your confirmation changes your son's perspective about you, gives him the confidence to fulfill his purpose, and reminds him that he's not in this on his own.

God is the perfect father because he

③ Rewards Purpose

Think about a time in your life when you challenged your son to perform a task you knew would be hard, but you promised him that if he did it, he would be rewarded. This happened even more so with Jesus. I mean, he existed in the very beginning, but he dropped his privileged heavenly status to become human. And that wasn't all. He experienced the following in his time on earth. He was—

>Born in a stable (Mark 3:20–21)
>
>Nearly murdered by Herod (Matthew 2:13–15)
>
>Followed by doubtful people (Mark 8:17–21)
>
>Persecuted by his own religious leaders (John 5:18)
>
>Torn with his own thoughts (Mark 14:32–39)
>
>Betrayed by a close follower (John 18:2–5)
>
>Embarrassed and humiliated (Matthew 26:67–68)
>
>Crucified for the whole world (Luke 23:33)
>
>Separated from God (Psalm 22:1)

Now, dads, can you seriously see asking your sons to do even a fourth of what God asked Jesus to do? I think not! God knew Jesus was the only one who could handle these tasks. Imagine: he did all this for us wicked, disobedient, prideful sinners. Jesus deserves to receive the greatest reward that ever can be given. What did God reward Jesus with? Here are just some of Jesus's rewards from God:

> Resurrection power (Matthew 28:18)
>
> All authority (Hebrews 2:8)
>
> High exaltation (Philippians 2:9–11)
>
> Ability to forgive sins (John 3:16)
>
> Mediator for us (1 Timothy 2:5–6)

Dads, honestly, after reading this chapter, do you feel that you come anywhere close to being a perfect father? Yeah, me neither. The good thing is that God knows we're weak. But we are also told to "[cast] all your care upon him; for he careth for you" (1 Peter 5:7 KJV).

Because God gave his Son, Jesus, purpose, confirmed that purpose, and rewarded that purpose, we can follow the same blueprint with our sons. I know I'm not the perfect dad, and maybe you've realized you're not, either. But, dads, can we do better, work harder, and pray to God to help us give, confirm, and reward purpose for our sons? You bet we can! I pray that God fills the void in our fatherhood practices right now toward our sons so that our sons will know and trust that when they do what is right by their natural father (us) or spiritual father (God), their suffering will never outweigh the rewards obedience brings. God is the *perfect father*!

Lessons I Learned

- In our own efforts, we are at best poor versions of the only perfect father, God.

- God is the perfect father because he exposed Jesus to his purpose and allowed him to fulfill his destiny. We must provide the same exposure for our sons.

- Because God gave his Son, Jesus, purpose, confirmed that purpose, and rewarded that purpose, we can follow that same blueprint with our sons every day.

Buddy Builder

Father, confess this to your son:

Son, I know I'm not perfect, but in my heart I desire to be a good father. I want to affirm and reassure you that I desire only what God wants for your life. I want you to forgive me for doing fatherhood my way and not God's way. From this day forward, I pledge these seven things by the grace of God:

1. I will stop being overcritical of your every move.

2. I promise to be present in the affairs of your life and not just in attendance.

3. I will set a godly example for you in all I do.

4. I will give you room to be you and will not overcrowd your space.

5. I will say no to your requests only for a purpose and not to harm you.

6. I will assure you daily through my attitude, words, and deeds that you are and always will be my MVP.

7. I will with God's help confirm and reward the gifts that God has given you.

Then remind yourself of this: *I am the perfect father— through God's grace. Amen!*

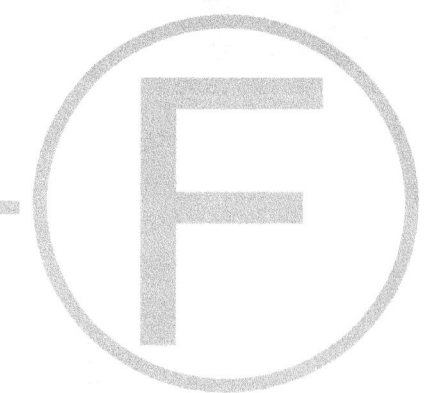

Father Talk

How important is it for a father to be an active part of his son's life?

FROM REVEREND ORD LIMBRICK, ENGINEER, RICHMOND, TEXAS:

I am the father of three boys that I have been given guardianship over by God. This guardianship involves helping, steering, and guiding them through childhood to manhood. This process requires me to be the parent, provider, priest, and protector. This is a big job and a big responsibility. Here are some examples:

1. Helping them with homework
2. Coaching their sport teams
3. Introducing them to Jesus Christ
4. Teaching them how to open their Bibles and find scriptures

5. Demonstrating to them how to worship and praise God

6. Teaching them to work (cut the yard, wash the car, and so on)

7. Disciplining them

8. Hugging them

9. Sharing with them my weaknesses and shortcomings

10. Teaching them how to treat and love a woman

FROM ANDRÉ L. KELLY, FORMER DEFENSIVE BACK COACH, PIKE HIGH SCHOOL, INDIANAPOLIS, INDIANA:

As a young African-American boy in Gary, Indiana, I didn't grow up with my father and rarely saw him. As I became a teenager, I was lucky to have my Uncle Barry, who was my father figure and male role model. I made a promise to my mother that when I had children, I would never treat them the way my father had treated me. I would always be a part of their lives no matter what.

In 1993 while in college, my first wife became pregnant with my daughter, Briana. Then two years later, she had my son, Brian. I knew I had to break the cycle of being an absentee father and keep my promise to my mom. Although my first wife and I divorced in 1997 and she had custody of my son, I made sure I was at every birthday party, school play, practice, and game.

I know fathers and father figures are important, because I learned from my Uncle Barry how a man is supposed to act, how to treat women, and to value education. I learned from God how a man should be committed to his children—no excuses! I have kept my promise. I was able to raise my son, Brian, to be a God-fearing, respectable young man. A father or a father figure is very important!

FROM CHRISTOPHER B. FISHER, HARRIS COUNTY SHERIFF'S OFFICE, RICHMOND, TEXAS:

As a child growing up in the southeast Bronx region of New York, I saw a lot of single-family homes that included Grandma and Grandpa or Mom and Grandma raising the children. This can still be the norm in the present day, but back in the 1980s and 1990s, it was my life.

Growing up, I knew my dad very well, but I was raised by my mother and grandparents. My father was fighting the demons in his life, so when he did come home, he was very unpleasant most of the time.

All my friends dealt with the same issue, or they didn't even have a father around. When I heard the older males outside the neighborhood talking and laughing about how many kids they had, I was bothered. I made it a point in my life that when I had kids, I was going to be a father, not just someone's dad.

That's why I keep God as the base foundation when it comes to raising my daughter. Always remember: anybody can be a dad, but being a father is a blessing! Love + time + faith in the Lord = fatherhood.

**FROM MARTY JOHNSON,
ATTORNEY AT LAW, OWNER OF BOUNDLESS GROWTH COACHING AND CONSULTING, BELLEVUE, WASHINGTON:**

My sons live in other cities now. My greatest reward is when they visit me, give me a hug, and say, "Dad, I love you so much." Their love stems from a relationship that began before they reached adulthood. God blessed me with the determination to have a relationship with my sons. Any man who has been through a pregnancy with his wife knows that a relationship with a child truly begins before the child is even born, just as God knew us before we were born (Jeremiah 1:5).

A father's role is not to lord over a son but to be a steadfast, life-long encourager and to foster his son's own creativity and natural talents. I've tried to be chief cheerleader for my boys with respect to any legitimate goal or dream they've wanted to pursue. A father's "being there" emotionally translates into a son's confidence in himself. Witness Derek Jeter's dad in the stands at so many games both before and long after Jeter became a star ballplayer.

Fathers demonstrate love for their sons by spending time with them. That starts with engaging with them at their level when they are young—literally playing games with them on the floor and showing them how to do and learn positive things. I think it is important for fathers to read to young children and to teach them how to read. Children absorb everything that goes on around them. Parents model behavior and values. Young boys view what their fathers do as important.

Every father is naturally positioned to have an impact on his son's self-image, self-esteem, and character. Fathers clearly help shape the men of tomorrow.

FROM GERALD SMITH, SR., MERCHANT MARINER, MERRILLVILLE, INDIANA:

Being active in your son's life is as important as breathing. You are the filter to the world for him. Train him in godly principles, not just reading the Bible but in acting according to its teachings as well. Show him how to be sensitive toward the things of God. Teach him to operate independently or as part of a team. Let him know where you went wrong and how you corrected your mistakes. Don't be ashamed to cry. Teach him how to stand firm in the midst of the storms of life. Make sure he knows the balance between continuing with what you start and realizing when things aren't for you.

Thank you for purchasing Better Father/Better Son

Hansen and Zion Harper are available for seminars, conferences, and key note speaking opportunities.

For more information please go to
www.betterfatherbetterson.com